A SPEL
FOR

COMMON WORDS FROM SENIOR PUPILS'
WRITTEN MATERIAL, SELECTED, GRADED
AND GROUPED FOR EASIER LEARNING

BY

FRED J. SCHONELL, Ph.D., D.Lit.

AND

GEORGE BROWN, M.A., F.E.I.S.

OLIVER AND BOYD

CONTENTS

INTRODUCTORY NOTE

This list of everyday words has been compiled by the authors after several years' study of the spelling errors made in the written material of pupils of ages 11 to 14+. The list thus represents in the main a minimum spelling vocabulary of additional common words for pupils up to 15 years of age.

The words have been divided into four groups. Group A contains easy words in which pupils are apt to make mistakes, while group C contains 345 longer words requiring careful attention to ensure their correct spelling.

Group B is composed of everyday words grouped according to similarity of structure so that pupils will be familiar with the common orthographic forms of these and similar (or derived) words as they arise during writing needs.

To ensure that common words listed in Groups A, B, and C are known out of their structural grouping or patterns, *some of those most frequently used in writing have been repeated in* Group D (*e.g.* beginning, guess, necessary). This device acts as a check and a revision.

For senior pupils the ordinary class spelling lesson should be but sparingly used—perhaps it serves a purpose only with weaker sections. For the most part, a list of words such as this is best used by supplying all pupils with copies and then allowing them to work in pairs as individual requirements determine. It is obvious that pupils should not be held up "learning" words they can already spell. As the spelling attainments of individual pupils vary in most classes by as much as five mental years, the pupils themselves can best determine their needs by testing each other with groups of words. Words not known can then be learnt and later recorded in a notebook.

The secret of success with a carefully compiled spelling list of everyday words which pupils need in their daily written work lies in its frequent quick use. Ten minutes' work, three or four times a week, will do much to improve the spelling of words used in all kinds of written English. By making the spelling of common words almost automatic we give the pupils confidence, for we thereby release extra energy for those constructive and imaginative aspects of English which demand full mental power and concentration.

F. J. S.
G. B.

GROUP A

184 Common Words often Wrongly Spelt

THE APOSTROPHE

| A boy's cap | A girl's hat | A week's holiday |
| Boys' caps | Girls' hats | Six weeks' holiday |

| A child's toys | A fox's den | The enemy's plans |
| Children's toys | Foxes' dens | The enemies' plans |

-ache	almost	because
again	already	been
among	altogether	beginning
answer	although	-believe
any	always	beneath

blue	cruel	colour
break	chimney	coming
busy	choose	cough
-business	coarse	could
bugle	hoarse	should
buy (*a badge*)	-ceiling	would

can't	dear	early
don't	doctor	easy
won't	does	either
o'clock	done	enough

5

farther (*away*)	garage	instead
forward	– grammar	just
flour	guess	know
flannel	guard	knows
fought	hear	knew
fourth	heard	laid
friend	half	– loose
grief	having	too (*much*)
grate (*fire*)	hour	two (2)

making	often	peace
many	one	pretty
meant	none	quick
minute	once	quiet
much	only	quietly
nearly	owe	cause
never	owner	caught

raise	(*to*) read	though
ready	soldier	thought
right	some	threw (*a stone*)
said	something	tired
says	straight	to-night
seems	sugar	trouble
separate	sure	truly
seize	surely	wear
scarcity	– sincerely	weather
since	appreciate	shrewdly

until	here	very
use	there	every
used	where	week
ugliness	– dissolve	genius

whether	women	dose
which	won (*a prize*)	lose
while	write	their
whose	writing	toothache
who	wrote	earache
whom	woolly	chosen
whole	woollen	towel
forty		through
quite	(*of*) course	tried

January	May	September
February	June	October
March	July	November
April	August	December

Sunday	Thursday	Spring
Monday	Friday	Summer
Tuesday	Saturday	Autumn
Wednesday		Winter

Group B

944 Common Words for Spelling Practice

anybody	everybody	somebody
anyone	everyone	someone
anything	everything	somewhere
anywhere	everywhere	sometimes
elsewhere		somehow

however	therefore	within
whatever	moreover	without
whenever	whole	withhold
wherever	which	withstand

forecast	overcoat	underhand
forefather	overcome	underneath
forehead	overlook	understand
foremost	overtake	undertake
forenoon	overthrow	undervalue
foresight	overrun	underrate

myself	ourselves	eastern
yourself	yourselves	western
himself	themselves	northern
herself		southern

agree	short	post
agreeable	shorter	postage
agreement	shorten	postal
disagree	shortage	postman
disagreeable	shortly	postmaster
conceit	measure	health
deceit	pleasure	stealth
receipt	treasure	wealth
bristle	nestle	bustle
thistle	trestle	hustle
whistle	wrestle	rustle
courage	image	necessary
encourage	imagine	necessitate
discourage	imagination	necessity
courageous	imaginable	necessitous
outrageous	imaginary	unnecessary
		necessarily
artillery	scullery	squadron
distillery	mystery	squander
cemetery	roguery	squalid
cutlery	scenery	square
machinery	monastery	squeal
action	inferior	feather
faction	superior	heather
fraction	interior	leather
traction	exterior	weather

album	careful	fulfil
altitude	doubtful	fulfilment
alter	fruitful	skilful
alteration	handful	wilful
alternate	plentiful	until
alternative	truthful	welcome
altogether	wonderful	welfare

collection	confession	adoption
connection	expression	attraction
direction	impression	exception
protection	oppression	exhibition
selection	possession	invention
construction	succession	relation
destruction	procession	separation
instruction	profession	suggestion

conclude	conclusion	conclusive
exclude	exclusion	exclusive
include	inclusion	inclusive

certify	paradise	brigadier
dignify	paragraph	cavalier
modify	paralysis	financier
notify	paralysed	gondolier
rectify	paramount	grenadier
simplify	parasite	bombardier

phantom	alphabet	atmosphere
phrase	asphalt	cenotaph
pheasant	emphasis	epitaph
photo	orphan	geography
photograph	pamphlet	telegraph
physique	prophet	telephone
cinematograph	nephew	saxophone
paragraph	semaphore	microphone
nymph	symphony	triumph
committee	auctioneer	beauteous
guarantee	engineer	courteous
jubilee	mountaineer	gorgeous
pedigree	mutineer	outrageous
referee	volunteer	righteous
rhyme	tyrant	sympathy
rhythm	tyranny	syringe
rhythmic	tyrannical	syrup
	tyrannous	system
acre	massacre	sepulchre
centre	meagre	sombre
fibre	sabre	spectre
lustre	sceptre	theatre
advertise	despise	exercise
chastise	devise	merchandise
comprise	disguise	supervise
criticise	enterprise	surprise

logic	music	optical
logical	musical	optician
magic	musician	electric
magical	physical	electrical
magician	physician	electrician

ough = o	*ough = off*	*ough = aw*
dough	cough	ought
though	trough	bought
although		brought

ough = uff	*ough = ow*	
enough	bough	fought
rough	plough	sought
tough	drought	thought
		wrought

autobiography	autogyro	automatic
autocrat	autograph	automobile

conceive	ceiling	caught
deceive	seize	taught
receipt	counterfeit	haughty
receive	weird	naughty
perceive	leisure	augury

neigh	eight	deign
sleigh	freight	reign
weigh	weight	foreign
neighbour	reindeer	sovereign

champion	chasm	arc
chariot	chaos	architect
choice	chemist	echo
charity	character	orchestra
chisel	Christian	scheme
chocolate	Christmas	scholar
church	choir	mechanic
avalanche	chorister	monarch*
cheque	chorus	patriarch

ardour	flavour	odour
armour	harbour	parlour
clamour	honour	valour
colour	humour	vapour
endeavour	labour	vigour

circumstance	accede	bus
circumstantial	concede	omnibus
circumference	intercede	syllabus
circumspect	precede	syllabuses
circumvent	recede	syllable

belief	believe	niece
relief	relieve	piece
brief	grieve	pier
grief	thieve	pierce
thief	achieve	priest
chief	reprieve	shriek
mischief	retrieve	siege

field	author	gaudy
shield	auction	laurel
wield	august	saucer
yield	autumn	sausage
gaunt	launch	chauffeur
haunt	laundry	restaurant
taunt	cauldron	somersault
gauntlet	cauliflower	tarpaulin
awful	hawthorn	exceed
awkward	lawful	proceed
awning	lawyer	succeed
yawning	tawdry	
beacon	breakfast	bower
reason	meadow	power
treason	pleasant	shower
wreath	threaten	tower
heathen	jealous	browse
sheathe	zealous	drowse
city	decent	justice
citizen	recent	notice
cinema	concert	office
cistern	glacier	juice
catch	ditch	flout
hatch	stitch	rout
patch	clutch	sprout
scratch	Dutch	stout
thatch	hutch	trout

almanac	automatic	graphic
lilac	chronic	lyric
maniac	critic	panic
topic	fabric	public
tropic	frantic	tunic
frolic	traffic	comedy
frolicking	trafficking	comedian
mimic	comic	tragedy
mimicking	comical	tragedian
picnic	tragic	politics
picnicking	tragical	politician
actor	creditor	sculptor
aggressor	debtor	spectator
ambassador	editor	surveyor
ancestor	emperor	survivor
bachelor	governor	traitor
censor	instructor	tailor
conductor	oppressor	translator
conqueror	orator	tutor
councillor	professor	warrior
curious	ferocious	generous
curiosity	ferocity	generosity
spacious	atrocious	intense
capacity	atrocity	intensity
sagacious	veracious	perverse
sagacity	veracity	perversity

eloquence	apologise	curio
eminence	authorise	curios
magnificence	compromise	photo
negligence	criticise	photos
penitence	economise	piano
prevalence	magnetise	pianos
prominence	advertise	studio
reverence	dramatise	studios
illustrious	ambitious	gracious
industrious	cautious	precious
studious	nutritious	spacious
tedious	superstitious	suspicious
victorious	delicious	bilious
diet	admirable	miracle
anxiety	desirable	obstacle
piety	durable	pinnacle
society	excitable	receptacle
variety	lovable	spectacle
gaiety	valuable	tabernacle
equator	angle	crumble
equality	bangle	jumble
equation	mangle	grumble
equable	tangle	tumble
estuary	strangle	stumble
article	continuous	scheme
particle	tempestuous	supreme
vehicle	virtuous	extreme

changeable
chargeable
marriageable
noticeable
peaceable
saleable
alphabetical
arithmetical

clerical
critical
historical
mystical
practical
typical
technical
adversary

hereditary
military
necessary
sanitary
secretary
solitary
tributary
voluntary

deficient
deficiency
proficient
proficiency
rebellion
separation

operation
provision
consult
consultation
expect
expectation

present
presentation
transport
transportation
deport
deportation

disable
disappear
disappoint
disapprove
discover
disgrace

association
celebration
desolation
devotion
execution
explosion

accusation
application
declaration
exclamation
explanation
exploration

dislike
dismiss
dispel
dispense
displace
display

illustration
investigation
sufficient
sufficiency
efficient
efficiency

multiplication
obligation
occupation
proclamation
reputation
revelation

A 2

cargo	potato	calf
cargoes	potatoes	calves
echo	tomato	loaf
echoes	tomatoes	loaves
hero	volcano	sheaf
heroes	volcanoes	sheaves
motto	negro	thief
mottoes	negroes	thieves
aggravate	disastrous	amiable
aggravation	mischievous	capable
anticipate	ponderous	formidable
anticipation	humorous	hospitable
exaggerate	vigorous	inimitable
exaggeration	strenuous	sociable
factory	blockade	descent
history	brigade	describe
ivory	comrade	deserter
memory	grenade	deserve
oratory	lemonade	desolate
theory	marmalade	desperate
territory	renegade	despondent
victory	serenade	destiny
audible	incredible	agitator
digestible	indelible	creator
divisible	invincible	moderator
forcible	contemptible	navigator
legible	irresponsible	operator
illegible	intelligible	radiator

bouquet	applause	expense
croquet	plausible	suspense
christen	liquor	cylinder
listen	liquid	cylindrical
cigar	colliery	martyr
cigarette	hosiery	martyrdom
censure	composure	expenditure
gesture	disclosure	manufacture
seizure	enclosure	signature

Words having silent letters :—

Silent ' b '	*Silent ' g '*	*Silent ' w*
bomb	gnat	wrangle
comb	gnash	wrap
crumb	gnaw	wrath
debt	sign	wreck
doubt	design	wrench
lamb	resign	wretch
tomb	ensign	wriggle
numb	consignment	wring
thumb	sleigh	wrinkle
plumber	neighbour	wrist
succumb	foreigner	sword
subtle	campaign	towards

Silent ' k '	*Silent ' l '*	*Silent ' n '*
knave	calm	autumn
knight	palm	column
knock	psalm	condemn
knowledge	salmon	hymn
knuckle	chalk	solemn

Silent ' h '

heir	rheumatism	aghast
honest	rhubarb	ghost
honour	rhythm	asthma
humour	shepherd	isthmus

Silent ' c '	*Silent ' s '*	*Silent ' u '*
scenery	aisle	guise
science	isle	guide
scissors	island	guilt
scythe	viscount	guard
muscle		guardian

Silent ' ue '

catalogue	vague	oblique
dialogue	rogue	opaque
fatigue	vogue	mosque
league	antique	grotesque
plague	unique	picturesque

GROUP C
345 Words for Special Attention

abolition
attraction
auctioneer
achievement
acknowledg(e)ment
acquaintance
admirable
admission
admittance
aerodrome

aeroplane
aeronautical
advertisement
agriculture
allotment
amiable
analysis
anxiety
apartments
anniversary

architecture
argument
armistice
artificial
artillery
assassin
assassinate
association
atmosphere
awkward

accommodation
accomplished
bachelor
balloon
banana
barbarous
battalion
bayonet
technical

barrage
behaviour
beneficial
benefited
besiege
bicycle
blizzard
career
campaign

cashier
casualties
catastrophe
cemetery
census
ceremony
character
carpenter
circuit

sympathy
system
tedious
telegram
testament

theatre
thorough
tobacco
viscount
volcano

welfare
wholesale
wholly
wizard
wretched

colleague
collier
collision
commemorate
commercial
committee
committed
concealed
conceited
conscious

criticism
conscience
conscientious
conclusion
condemned
conspicuously
conqueror
correspondence
corridor
courageous

courtesy
courteous
crystal
colonel
column
cuckoo
curiosity
cylinder
deceitful
decision

definitely
descendant
descent
ascent
desperate
develop
dialogue
diameter
dictionary
diphtheria

disagreeable
disappointed
discipline
earnestly
efficiently
Egyptian
electricity
exclamation
embarrassing
alacrity

exhausted
expensive
explanation
extraordinary
extremely
fatigue
ferocious
fiery
aggressor
siren

democracy
disease
endeavour
enterprise
enthusiasm
especially
European
exaggeration
expense
efficiency

foreigners
fulfil
gases
generosity
gorgeous
gossiping
government
gracious
grandeur
grammar

grievance
grievous
guardian
guinea
gymnastics
harassing
horizon
horizontal
humiliation
judicious

humorous
illegal
imaginary
inaccessible
incurred
influenza
ingenious
spacious
insensible
inseparable

abyss
accessories
bureau
bronchitis
catarrh
chronic
centenary
cortege
debris
initial

incandescent
manœuvre
mediæval
neuralgia
camouflage
plateau
pneumonia
rendezvous
immense
massacre

mysterious
rheumatism
souvenir
inseparable
intelligence
judg(e)ment
juveniles
knuckle
language
leisure

mosquito
libraries
lieutenant
luggage
luncheon
luxurious
magnificent
memoranda
merchandise
merciful

mischievous
miserable
mistletoe
muscles
museum
navies
necessary
nineteenth
nobility
obstacle

neutrality
nonsense
nuisance
occasionally
occupation
occurrence
operation
orchestra
parliament

omitted
official
paraffin
parallel
peaceable
peaceably
precision
preferred
privilege

opportunity
quarrelsome
quarrelling
peculiar
perceive
persevere
perseverance
persuade
persuasion

procedure	Protestant	melancholy
petroleum	psalms	pigeon
physical	razor	porridge
procession	rebellion	possessed
proclamation	receipt	possession
profited	receiving	possible
programme	recompense	practical
pronunciation	recruit	(to) practise
prophecy	referring	preceded
precipice	righteous	preceding
release	romance	sheriff
reliable	scarcely	similar
religious	scheme	tobacconist
vicious	scholarly	tourist
reputation	scientific	tragedy
resemblance	scissors	relying
revelation	secrecy	treasury
ridiculous	secretary	trivial
repetition	seizing	twelfth
typical	squeeze	treacherous
tyrannous	suburbs	vigorous
unconscious	successful	virtuous
unusually	sufficient	villainy
sincerity	vapour	suspicious
skilful	vegetables	woollen
slaughter	vehicle	yacht
innocence	veil	wearisome
spiritual	vengeance	vanities

emphasis	parliamentary	pierced
glazier	paraphrase	sovereign
inclemency	eulogy	passionate
pacifist	surgeon	zero

GROUP D

3136 Common Words

abate	✓abundance	✓accommodate
abating	abundant	accommodation
ability	abuse	accompany
abolition	accelerate	accompaniment
abrupt	acceleration	accompanist
abruptly	accelerator	approach
✓absence	accept	approve
absent	acceptance	✓approval
abolish	acceptable	ardent

accomplish	bargain	almost
accomplishment	battalion	alphabet
according	battery	alphabetically
accordingly	bayonet	already
account	access	altogether
accurate	accession	although
accuracy	accident	almanac
✓accusation	✓accidental	almond
accustom	athletic	alert

Atlantic	adjourn	agile
amount	admire	agility
amuse	admiration	agitate
amusement	admirable	agitation
amusing	admit	agony
analyse	✓admittance	agonise
✓analysis	admission	addition
ancestor	adopt	additional
ancient	adoption	address

angel	appal	apply
angelic	−✗appalling	applied
✓anonymous	apparatus	applicant
✓Antarctic	apparel	✓application
anticipate	apparent	applaud
✓anticipation	appeal	applause
anywhere	appear	appointment
anxiety	✓appearance	✓appreciate
✗anxious	appetite	appreciation

attach	arrange	beauty
attachment	disarrange	beautiful
attend	✓arrangement	beauteous
attendance	arrest	artillery
✓attendant	arrive	artisan
attention	arrival	ascent
attract	arrogant	ascend
attraction	arrogance	ascension
attractive	✓amateur	ascertain

acquire
acquisition
acquisitive
acquit
acquitted
acquittal
adieu
adjective
adjacent

anchor
anecdote
angle
angular
angler
angry
angrily
ankle
Asia

advance
advancement
advantage
advantageous
adventure
adventurous
advertise
advertisement
article

150

advise
advisable
aerial
aeroplane
affair
affection
affectionate
afford
ageing

beach
beacon
acre
actual
actually
acute
ache
aching
artificial

balloon
ballot
balloted
banana
amazement
agreeable
agreement
agriculture
agriculturist

allege
allot
allotment
allow
allowance
ally
alliance
aggravate
aggravation

arbitrate
arbitration
architect
architecture
Arctic
argument
arithmetic
apartment
apostrophe

abbot
abbey
ambassador
ambiguity
ambiguous
ambition
ambitious
America
amiable

assail   assent   academy
assailant   associate   achieve
assassin   association   achievement
assassinate   assume   acid
assault   assumption   acidity
assist   assure   acknowledge
assistance   assurance   acknowledg(e)ment
assistant   armistice   acquaint
assigned   armour   acquaintance

bacon   auspices   autumn
baggage   Australia   avalanche
balance   author   avenue
auction   authoress   average
auctioneer   authorise   aviation
attitude   authority   aviator
attempt   authoritative   avoid
audience   automatic   avoidable
August   automobile   awaiting

awe   bandage   writing
awful   barbarian   written
awry   barbarous   apprehend
awestruck   bachelor   wrongful
awkward   alacrity   wrought
astonish   album   yacht
astonishment   alcohol   yeoman
asylum   alien   yeomanry
atmosphere   ammunition   yield

beckon
beginning
behave
behaviour
belief
believe
−×believable
×besiege
belligerent

benefit
−×benefited
benefiting
beneficial
benevolent
benevolence
bequeath
bequest
√bazaar

beseech
besought
beverage
bewilder
bewilderment
bicycle
biscuit
billiards
√biography

blizzard
blue
bluish
boatswain
boisterous
bomb
booty
borrow
barrel

boundary
breadth
√breath
breathe
breakfast
brethren
briar
√brief
brevity

brilliant
brilliance
bristle
brooch
√bruise
budget
build
builder
building

Britain
British
bulletin
burden
√bureau
burglar
bury
buried
burial

bus
√buses
busy
busily
√business
butcher
bugle
bulwark
beech tree

cabinet
calamity
calamitous
calculate
calculation
calendar
calico
calmly
calmness

camera
✓ campaign
Canada
Canadian
canal
candid
candidly
cancel
✓ cancelled

candidate
canoe
canopy
canvass
canvassing
canvasser
capable
✓ capability
capacity

captain
✓ career
careful
✓ carefully
carefulness
cargo
cargoes
carol
carpenter

carrot
cabbage
cannibal
carrying
✓ carriage
carrier
cartridge
cash
cashier

catalogue
cataract
✓ catastrophe
catechism
caterpillar
cathedral
cauliflower
caution
cavalry

✓ cautious
cautiously
cease
ceaseless
✓ ceiling
celebrate
celebration
celebrity
✓ cemetery

censure
census
centre
central
✓ century
✓ ceremony
ceremonial
certain
certainly

certify
certificate
challenge
challenger
champion
championship
change
changing
—✗changeable

chasm
chaos
✓ character
characteristic
charity
charitable
chastise
chastisement
✓ chauffeur

chemist
chemistry
chestnut
✓cheque
chieftain
children
chimney
China
Chinese

chisel
chivalry
chivalrous
chocolate
choice
choir
choked
chord
chorus

Christian
Christmas
chronicle
cigarette
cinders
cipher
circle
circular
✓circuit

circumference
circumstance
circus
cistern
cinema
channel
funnel
citizen
citizenship

civil
civility
civilian
✓civilise
civilisation
clamour
clamorous
clean
cleanliness

clear
clearance
clergyman
client
clothes
coarse
cocoa
coal
clause

collapse
collapsible
collect
collection
college
collide
collision
collier
colliery

colonel
colony
colonies
colonial
✓colossal
colour
column
combine
combination

comedy
comedian
comedienne
comic
comical
coming
collar
✓colleague
collector

commence
commencement
✓commemorate
commemoration
commerce
commercial
commit
✓committed
committee

company
companion
compare
comparative
comparison
compass
compassion
compel
compelled

compulsion
complain
complaint
complete
completion
complicate
complication
compliment
✓complimentary

comply
compliance
compose
composition
comprehend
comprehension
compress
compression
compromise

comrade
conceal
concealed
conceit
conceited
conceive
✓conceivable
concentrate
concentration

concern
concerning
concert
concise
concisely
conclude
conclusion
condemn
condemnation

condense
condensation
✓condescend
condescension
condition
conditional
conduction
conductor
confer

conference
conferred
confess
confession
confident
confidence
confuse
confusion
congratulate

congratulation
congregate
congregation
conjure
conjurer
connect
connection
conquer
conqueror

conscience
conscientious
conscious
consciousness
consent
consequent
consequence
conjunction
convoy

consider
consideration
consign
consignment
consist
consistent
console
consolation
consonant

conspicuous
constable
constrain
constraint
construct
construction
consume
consumer
consumption

contemplate
contemplation
contempt
contemptible
contemptuous
continent
continental
contradict
contradiction

contrary
control
controlled
contribute
contribution
convention
co-operate
co-operation
co-operator

convenient
convenience
converse
conversation
conversationalist
convey
conveyance
convict
conviction

contract
contractor
copious
cordial
cordially
corporation
course
courtesy
courteous

correction
correspond
correspondence
correspondent
corridor
corrupt
corruption
costume
convince

couch
cough
council
councillor
country
countries
couple
courageous
concussion

cousin
covenant
covenanter
cover
covetous
covetousness
coward
cowardice
crayon

create
creator
creation
creature
credit
creditable
creditor
crime
criminal

✓ crescent
✓ crisis
crises
critic
critical
criticise
✓ criticism
cruel
cruelty

crusade
crusader
crystal
crystallise
cunning
cupboard
curator
curious
curiously
✓ curiosity

currant (*fruit*)
curtain
curtsy
curtsying
cushion
custom
customer
✓ customary
cycle
✓ cyclist

cyclone
cypress
cylinder
✓ cylindrical
current
currency
(*Queen's*) Counsel
counsellor
(*adviser*)
cause

common
commonwealth
commotion
✓ community
communion
crowd
✓ cuckoo
cutlery
condone

daily
dainty
dairy
damage
debate
debating
✓ debatable
debt
✓ debtor

deceive
–✗ deceit
deceitful
deception
decease
decent
decency
decide
decisive

✓decimal
declare
✓declaration
decorate
decoration
✓decrease
defect
defective
✓deficient

defend
defence
defer
deferred
deference
define
definite
—✗definitely
definition

defraud
defy
defiance
degrade
degradation
daughter
December
dearth
decline

dejected
dejection
distribute
distribution
deliberate
deliberation
delicate
✓delicious
delicacy

deliver
delivery
✓deliverance
delude
delusion
demonstrate
demonstration
dense
density

deny
denial
depart
departure
department
depend
dependable
✓dependent
depth

deposit
depositor
depot
deputation
derive
derivation
descend
descent
✓descendant

describe
description
descriptive
desert
desertion
deserter
design
designation
derelict

desire
✓desirable
desirous
despair
—✗desperate
desperation
destination
destroy
destruction

despise	develop	diagram
demolish	developing	dialogue
detach	✗development	✓diameter
detachment	device	diamond
detect	devote	diary
detective	devotion	dictionary
detector	devour	differ
determined	dexterity	different
determination	diagonal	difference

difficult	diligent	disappear
difficulty	diligence	✗disappearance
digest	diminish	disappoint
digestible	direct	disappointment
digestion	direction	dismay
digit	director	disaster
dignity	disagree	disastrous
dignified	✓disagreeable	disciple
detail	disagreement	✓discipline

discount	disease	disorder
discourage	disfigure	dishonour
✓discourteous	disfigurement	dispatch
discover	✓disguise	dispel
discovery	dismiss	dispense
discreet	dismissal	dispensation
discretion	disobey	dispersion
discuss	disobedient	displease
✓discussion	✓disobedience	displeasure

distinct
distinctly
distinction
distinguish
distribute
distribution
district
disturb
disturbance

divide
division
divisible
divisor
dividend
divine
domestic
dominion
doubtful

dough
drought
drudgery
duchess
dull
dullness *or*
  dulness
duly
duration

dye
dyeing
dyer
dissent
dissension
dissipate
dissipation
dissolve
dissolution

dwarf
eager
early
earlier
earliest
earnest
earnestly
earthquake
earthenware

eccentric
echo
eclipse
economy
economic
economical
Edinburgh
editor
edition

educate
education
effect
effective
efficient
efficiency
effort
Egypt
Egyptian

eight
eighty
eightieth
eighteen
either
eject
effigy
elaborate
elaboration

elastic
elasticity
elect
election
electric
electricity
electrician
elegant
elegance

elapse
eloquent
eloquence
embarrass
embarrassing
embezzle
emergency
emigrate
emigration

emigrant
eminent
eminence
emphasise
emphasis
emphatic
employer
employee
employment

empty
emptied
enclose
enclosing
enclosure
encore
encourage
encouragement
endeavour

endure
endurance
enemy
enemies
energy
energies
energetic
engage
engagement

engine
engineer
enjoy
enjoyment
enlighten
enlightenment
enormous
enough
enrol

enrolling
enterprise
entertain
entertainment
enthusiasm
enthusiastic
entice
enticement
entitle

entrust
entire
entirely
envy
envies
envelop (*verb*)
enveloping
envelope (*noun*)
epidemic

escape
especially
equal
equally
equality
equator
equip
equipment
equivalent

era
erect
erection
episode
epitaph
essay
essence
essential
essentially

establish
establishment
estate
esteem
estimate
estimation
estuary
eternity
evacuate

evaporate
evaporation
evident
evidence
exact
exaggerate
exaggeration
examine
examination

exceed
exceedingly
excel
excellence
except
exception
excess
excessive
errand

exchange
exchangeable
exchequer
excise
excite
excitement
exciting
excitable
exercise

exclaim
exclamation
exclude
exclusion
excuse
excusable
execute
execution
executive

excursion
exertion
exhaustion
exhausted
exhibit
exhibition
exhibitor
exist
existence

fiery
figure
figurative
film
finance
financial
financier
final
finally

flannel
flavour
flourish
folk
foolish
force
forcible
forefather
forecast

foreign
foreigner
foreman
foresee
foretell
forewarn
forfeit
forgive
forgiving

external
extinct
extinction
extinguish
extract
extraction
extraordinary
extravagant
extravagance

extreme
extremely
extremity
faction
factory
factories
failure
fairy
fairies

falsehood
family
familiar
famine
fancy
fancied
fanciful
fascinate
fascination

fashion
fashionable
fatal
fatality
fasten
fastening
fathom
fatigue
favour

favourable
favourite
feather
feature
February
feign
feigned
fellowship
ferocious

ferocity
fertile
fertility
festive
festival
festivity
fidelity
fierce
fiercely

expand
expansion
expansive
expedition
expectation
expend
expenditure
expense
expensive

experience
experiment
experimental
expire
expiration
explain
explanation
explode
explosion

explore
exploration
expose
exposure
exquisite
extend
extension
extensive
exterior

forget
forgotten
fortunate
fortunately
forward
foundry
fowl
fraction
fragment

fragrant
fragrance
fraud
fraudulent
freedom
frequent
frequence
famous
fever

friction
fright
frighten
frightful
frigid
fugitive
fulfil
fulfilment
fulfilling

funeral
furnace
furniture
furtive
fury
furious
future
fruit
fruiterer

gaiety
gaily
garage
gardener
garrison
gas
gases
gauge
general

generate
generation
generous
generosity
genius
genteel
gentle
gentleman
genuine

geography
geographical
geology
geological
gesture
ghastly
ghost
giant
gigantic

gipsy
gipsies
glacier
glamour
glamorous
glazier
goal
goddess
gorgeous

gossip
gossiping
govern
government
governor
gracefully
gracious
gradual
gradually

grammar
✓ grammatical
gramophone
grandeur
granite
grateful
gratify
gratitude
gravity

Greece
greedy
greediness
greet
greeting
grief
grieve
grievous
✓ grievance

grocer
groceries
grotesque
growth
grudge
grudgingly
guarantee
guard
guardian

guess
guessing
guest
guide
guiding
guidance
guild
guilt
guilty

guinea
gymnastics
handful
handfuls
handkerchiefs
handle
happened
harass
harassing

hardihood
harbour
harmony
harmonious
hasten
hastily
hatred
haughty
haughtiness

haul
hauling
havoc
hazard
hazardous
hazy
haziness
✓ headache
headquarters

healthy
healthiness
hearth
heather
heathen
height
heighten
heir
heiress

hero
✓ heroes
heroine
heroic
heroism
hesitate
hesitation
hideous
hoarse

hobby
hobbies
hoist
hoisted
honour
honourable
honorary
hoping
horizon

horizontal
horrible
horrify
horror
hospital
hospitality
✓humour
✓humorous
humorist

hundred
hundredth
hurricane
hurry
hurried
hurriedly
hustle
human
humanity

hymn
✓hypocrite
ice
icicle
iciness
icing
ideal
idealise
✓idealistic

identify
identification
independent
independence
idiot
idiotic
ignore
ignorance
ignorant

✓illegible
illuminate
illumination
illusion
illustrate
illustration
imagine
imagination
✓imaginary

imitate
✓imitation
immortal
illegal
impartial
impatient
impatience
imperative
impertinent

impertinence
impetus
impetuous
impossible
✓impossibility
impress
impression
imprison
imprisonment

improve
✓improvement
impudent
impudence
impulse
impulsive
✓inaccessible
incapacity
incense

incessant
incident
incidental
incidentally
include
inclusion
inclusive
income
incompetent

inconvenient
inconvenience
increase
increasing
incur
incurred
indefinite
independent
independence

India
Indian
indifferent
indifference
indignant
indignation
individual
indolent
indolence

indulge
indulgence
indulgent
industry
industries
industrious
infect
infection
infectious

infer
inference
inferior
influence
influential
influenza
ingenious
ingenuity
inhabit

inhabitant
inherit
inheritance
initial
initialed
initialing
injure
injury
injurious

liberal
liberality
library
libraries
librarian
licence (*noun*)
lieutenant
lighten
lightening

likeable
liking
likelihood
limb
linen
lining
linoleum
liquid
liquorice

listener
lively
livelihood
local
locality
locomotive
lodge
lodging
lodger

insure
insurance
intellect
intellectual
intelligent
intelligence
intense
intensive
intention

interesting
interfere
interference
interior
interval
intimate
intimation
invade
invasion

intoxicate
intoxication
introduce
introduction
intrude
intrusion
interrupt
interruption
invalid

invaluable
invent
invention
inventor
investigate
investigation
invigorate
invisible
invite

invitation
irregular
irregularity
irritate
irritable
irritation
island
issue
issuing

ivory
immediate
immediately
immense
immensely
immovable
January
Japan
Japanese

jealous
jealousy
jeopardy
jester
jewel
jeweller
jewellery
journal
journalist

journey
journeys
jubilee
judge
judg(e)ment
juice
juicy
junction
junior

justice
justify
justification
juvenile
innocent
innocence
innovation
item
keel

keen	knitting	laboratory
keenness	knot	lament
kennel	knowledge	lamentable
khaki	knuckle	lamentation
kindred	label	landscape
knapsack	labelling	language
knave	labour	languid
knead	labourer	lantern
knight	laborious	latitude
laudable	lecture	leisure
laugh	lecturer	legitimate
laughter	ledger	length
kernel	legacy	lengthen
launch	legend	leopard
laundry	legion	lettuce
lawful	legislate	level
lawyer	legislation	levelled
league	legislator	liable
inquiry	insolent	institute
inscribe	insolence	institution
inscription	inspect	instruct
inseparable	inspection	instruction
insensible	inspector	instructor
insert	instalment	instrument
insertion	instance	insular
insist	instantly	insult
insistence	instinct	insulting

lonely
loneliness
longitude
luggage
lose
loser
lovely
loveliness
lozenge

loose
luncheon
luscious
lustre
lustrous
luxury
luxurious
lightning (*flash*)
literature

license (*verb*)
machine
machinery
machinist
magazine
magic
magical
magician
miserable

magistrate
magnet
magnetic
magnetise
magnetism
magnificent
maintain
maintenance
mallet

majesty
majestic
major
majority
manage
manageable
management
maniac
manners

mantelpiece
manual
manufacture
manufacturer
margarine
margin
marine
mariner
meadow

market
marketing
martial
marvel
marvelled
marvellous
massacre
massive
material

mathematics
marriage
meagre
meagrely
mayor
measles
measure
measurer
measurement

mechanic
mechanical
medicine
Mediterranean
melancholy
melody
melodious
mention
mentioned

mere	migrate	**minor**
merely	migration	minority
mercy	military	minstrel
merciful	militarism	minstrelsy
merciless	murmur	minute
message	murmuring	miracle
messenger	mimic	miraculous
metropolis	mimicking	museum
microscope	miniature	miscellaneous
mischief	modify	moreover
mischievous	modification	mosque
modern	moisture	mosquito
mistake	money	motto
mistakable	moneys	mottoes
mistletoe	monster	mould
misuse	monstrous	movable
model	moral	moving
modelled	morality	monarch
mourn	muscle	mystery
mournful	muscular	mysterious
mouthful	musical	mission
mouthfuls	musician	missionary
multiply	mutiny	missile
multiplier	mutineer	narrate
multiplication	mutual	narration
million	mutually	narrative
millionaire	mirror	naughty

national
nationalism
navy
navies
necessary
necessarily
necessity
negative
nephew

neglect
neglectful
negligence
negligible
neighbour
neighbourhood
neither
nerve
nervous

nicety
niche
nine
ninety
nineteenth
nobility
noise
noiseless
nonsense

noticeable
notify
notification
nourish
nourishment
novel
novelty
nuisance
numerous

nursery
nymph
niece
oasis
oases
obey
obeyed
obedience
obedient

obituary
object
objection
oblige
obliged
obligation
obscure
obstacle
obstinate

obtuse
obvious
obviously
occasion
occasionally
occupy
occupied
occupier
occupation

occur
occurred
occurring
occurrence
odour
odorous
offend
offence
offensive

officer
official
omit
omitted
omitting
omission
omnibus
omnibuses
oneself

ocean
o'clock
oculist
onion
opaque
operate
operation
operator
opinion

origin
original
originally
ornament
ornamental
orphan
orphanage
ought
ounce

parachute
paralyse
paralysis
paraphrase
parcel
parchment
pardon
pardonable
parliament

opponent
opportunity
oppose
opposite
opposition
oppress
oppression
oppressor
ostrich

outrage
outrageous
oyster
Pacific
pagan
paganism
pageant
palace
pamphlet

particular
particularly
philosophy
partnership
passable
passenger
passion
pasteurise
paternal

optimism
optimist
orchard
orchestra
orchestral
ordeal
ordinary
organise
organisation

panic
panicky
pantomime
parable
parade
paraffin
parallel
paralleled
parallelogram

patience
patient
patriot
patriotic
pause
peace
peaceable
peaceably
peaceful

peasant peninsula perfume
peculiar penitent perforate
peered pasture perhaps
penalty pattern period
penance perambulator periodical
pencil perceive peril
pendant perceiving perilous
penetrate perimeter permanent
penetration perennial permanence

pension persist phantom
permit persistence pheasant
permitting person photograph
permission personal photographer
perpetual persuade phrase
perpetually persuasion physical
persevere perverse physically
persevering pessimist physician
perseverance petroleum ✓ physique

pincers piece pioneer
piano pier pistol
pianos pierce pity
picnic piety pitiful
picnicking pious piteous
picture pigeon pitiless
picturesque pilot placid
penny piloting plague
penniless pinafore plainness

planet
pleasant
pleasure
pleasurable
plough
ploughman
plumber
pneumatic
pneumonia

poet
poetry
poetical
poison
poisonous
policeman
policy
politics
political

popular
popularity
population
porcelain
portion
portrait
portraiture
position
positive

pledge
possess
possession
possessor
possible
possibility
postpone
postponement
postscript

porridge
potato
potatoes
poultice
poultry
pounce
poverty
practice (*noun*)
practical

prairie
prayer
precaution
precede
preceding
precedence
precious
precipice
precipitous

precise
precisely
precision
predecessor
predict
prediction
prefer
preferred
preference

prejudice
preliminary
premises
premium
prepare
preparation
prescribe
prescription
present

presence
preside
president
presume
presumption
pressure
pretend
pretence
priest

pretext   principal (*chief*)   profit
prevail   private   profiting
prevalent   privilege   profiteer
prevalence   probable   proclaim
prevent   probably   proclamation
prevention   probability   produce
previous   proceed   production
previously   procession   progress
primary   prodigal   progressive

profess   prompt   prophet
profession   promptitude   prophecy (*noun*)
professor   pronounce   proportion
project   pronouncement   promote
projection   pronunciation   promotion
prominent   propel   prosecute
prominence   propelling   prosecution
promise   propeller   prospect
promising   proprietor   prospective

prosperous   provision   punctual
prostrate   province   punctuality
prostration   provincial   puncture
protect   provoke   punishment
protector   provoking   purchase
protection   provocation   purchasing
provide   publish   purify
provident   publisher   purpose
providence   publication   purposeful

pursue
pursuing
pursuit
puzzle
pylon
pyramid
prophesy (*verb*)
programme
psalm

quadruped
qualify
qualification
quantity
quantities
quarrel
quarrelled
quarrelling
quarrelsome

quaint
quarry
quay
quality
quench
quest
question
queue
quiet

quote
quotation
quotient
radiant
radiator
radiance
radical
radius
radii (*plural*)

raiment
rally
random
ransom
rapid
rapidity
rare
rarely
rarity

ratio
razor
ready
readily
readiness
really
reason
reasonable
realise

rebel
rebelled
rebellion
rebuke
receive
receiving
reception
receipt
rectangle

recent
recently
recipe
recite
recitation
reckon
reckoning
recognise
recognition

recoil
recollect
recollection
recommend
reconcile
reconciliation
reduce
reducing
reducible

reduction
refer
referring
reference
referee
reflect
reflection
reflector
recruit

refuge
refugee
regard
regarding
regiment
register
registrar
regret
regrettable

regular
regularity
rehearse
rehearsal
reign (*of king*)
region
rejoice
rejoicing
recompense

relate
relating
relation
relative
relax
relaxation
release
reliable
reliability

relief
relieve
religion
religious
relying
reluctant
reluctance
remainder
reprieve

rein (*for horse*)
remedy
remember
remembrance
remit
remitting
remittance
remorse
remorseful

removable
removal
renounce
renunciation
renown
repair
repeat
repetition
reserve

repel
repulsion
represent
representation
repute
reputation
reptile
request
require

rescue
rescuing
resemble
resemblance
resent
resentful
reside
residence
missile

resign
resignation
respect
respectful
respectfully
responsible
responsibility
resolve
residue

resolute
resolution
resource
response
responsive
restaurant
restraint
resume
resumption

retrieve
retriever
reveal
revelation
revenue
revere
reverent
revive
revival

revolve
revolt
revolution
rheumatism
rhubarb
rhyme
rhythm
ridicule
ridiculous

ribbon
rifle
righteous
righteousness
riot
riotous
rival
rivalling
rivalry

robbery
rogue
roguery
roguish
romance
romantic
rout (*defeat*)
route (*road*)
rubbish

ruffle
rumour
Russia
Russian
sacrament
sacred
sacrifice
saddle
saddler

safeguard
safety
salad
salary
salaries
salmon
salute
salutation
sandals

sandwich
satisfy
satisfied
satisfaction
satisfactory
Saturday
saucepan
saucer
saucy

sausage

savings

saviour

scaffold

scandal

scandalous

scarce

scarcely

scarcity

scarlet

scene

scenery

scent

scented

scheme

schedule

scholar

scholarly

science

scientific

scientist

scissors

scorch

scribble

sculptor

sculpture

scythe

search

season

seasonable

secret

secrecy

secretary

section

secure

security

seize

seizing

seizure

select

selection

senate

senator

senior

sentence

sense

sensation

sensible

sensibility

sensitive

sensitivity

separate

separately

separation

sergeant

sentinel

serious

seriously

service

serviceable

settle

settler

settlement

several

severe

severely

severity

shepherd

sheriff

shoes

shoeing

shoemaker

shoulder

shield

session

shrewd

shrewdness

shriek

shrieking

shrubbery

siege

sign	single	skeleton
signed	singular	slaughter
signal	siren	slight
signature	sirloin	slippery
similar	situation	snatch
similarity	skill	social
sincere	skilful	sociable
sincerely	skirmish	socialism
sincerity	slander	society
sneeze	solve	special
shining	soluble	specially
solemn	solution	specimen
solemnity	soothe	spectacle
solicit	soothing	spectator
solicitor	sovereign	speech
solicitude	Spain	speechless
solitary	Spaniard	soul
solitude	Spanish	source
sphere	squirrel	stitch
spherical	standard	stomach
splendid	statement	straight
splendour	stationer	strength
sponge	stationery (*paper*)	strengthen
spoonful	steadfast	strenuous
spoonfuls	stealth	stroll
squeal	stealthily	strolled
squeeze	stillness	struggle

stubborn
study
student
studious
stupidity
style
stylish
subdue
subduing

submit
submitted
submission
subscribe
subscription
substitute
substitution
subtle
subtlety

subtraction
suburb
suburban
succeed
success
successful
succession
successive
successor

subsequent
succour
sufficient
sugar
suggest
suggestion
suicide
suitable
suitability

stationary (*fixed*)
sulphur
sultry
summit
summon
superintend
superintendent
superior
superiority

supply
supplies
suppose
supposition
supreme
supremacy
surface
surgeon
surgery

surplus
surprise
surprising
survey
surveying
surveyor
survive
survival
survivor

suspect
suspicion
suspicious
suspense
sustain
swollen
syllable
surrender
surround

symbol
sympathy
sympathetic
sympathise
symptom
synagogue
system
systematic
syringe

syrup
tabernacle
tactics
tailor
tailoring
talent
talented
tapestry
tariff

tarpaulin
taunt
tease
teasing
technical
technique
tedious
teetotal
teetotaller

telegraph
telegram
telephone
telescope
temperate
temperance
temperature
temporary
temptation

tenant
tendency
tendencies
tennis
terrible
terrier
terrify
terrified
terrific

territory
territorial
terror
testament
testimony
testimonial
theatre
theatrical
theory

therefore
thermometer
thief
thieves
thieving
thigh
thimble
thirsty
thirteen

thirty
thistle
thought
thoughtful
thoughtfulness
thoughtless
thumb
thwart
thwarted

thorough
thoroughly
thoroughness
tinge
tingeing
tiresome
tobacco
tobaccos
tobacconist

toboggan
tomato
tomatoes
to-morrow
tongue
tonic
toothache
topic
topical

torment
torrent
torrential
tortoise
torture
touch
touched
tourist
towards

traditional
traffic
trafficking
tragedy
tragic
tragedian
traitor
traitorous
together

tranquil
tranquillity
transact
transaction
transcribe
transcription
transfer
transferred
transform

translate
translation
transparent
transport
transportation
transpose
travel
traveller
travelling

treachery
treacherous
treasure
treasurer
treasury
tremendous
trespass
trespassing
trespasser

treaty
treatment
tribute
tributary
tricycle
triumph
triumphant
trivial
triviality

tropic
tropics
tropical
trifle
trough
trousers
truant
truancy
truncheon

truly
trustworthy
Tuesday
tuition
tutor
tutoring
tunnel
twelfth
Turkey

twilight
type
typewriter
typist
tyrant
tyranny
tyrannous
ugly
ugliness

umbrella	unusual	urge
umpire	unusually	urgent
uncle	union	urgency
unconscious	unique	usage
uncouth	universe	useful
undaunted	universal	usefulness
unfortunate	university	utter
ungrateful	upheaval	uttered
unnecessary	utensil	utterance
vacant	valley	vase
vacancy	valleys	vault
vacation	value	vegetables
vagrant	valuable	vegetation
vagrancy	vary	vehement
vague	varied	vehicle
valiant	variety	vengeance
vapour	varieties	ventilate
valour	various	ventilation
veil	vice	vigour
venture	vicious	vigorous
verdict	victim	village
verify	vessel	villain
verification	victory	villainy
vertical	victories	vinegar
veteran	victorious	violent
vicar	victuals	violence
vicarage	view	violet

virtue
virtuous
visitor
vision
visible
visibility
vocation
vocational
volcano
volcanoes

weather
Wednesday
weigh
weight
welcome
welfare
whisper
whistle
whooping-cough
whose

wizard
worsted
wrangle
wrap
wrapping
wrath
wrathful
wreck
wreckage

volley
volleys
volume
volunteer
vowel
vulgar
vulgarity
waistcoat
weapon
warrior

whole
wholly
wholesale
wholesome
wield
whether
which
whither
whirl
whirling

writhe
wreath
wrench
wrestle
wrestler
wretch
wretched
wrinkle
wrist

wary
warily
wayfarer
wayfaring
wealth
wealthy
wealthier
weary
wearily
weariness

witch
witness
woe
woeful
wonder
wondrous
wool
woolly
woollen
wilful

yolk (*egg*)
youth
youthful
zeal
zealous
zero
zest
zigzag
zone

OLIVER & BOYD
Robert Stevenson House
1–3 Baxter's Place
Leith Walk
Edinburgh EH1 3BB

A division of Longman Group Ltd.

ISBN 0 05 000406 9

First published 1940
Nineteenth Impression 1979

Printed in Hong Kong by
Wilture Enterprises (International) Ltd